C000291776

LOVE SIGNS

Jonathan Cainer

PIATKUS

Also in this series
LOVE POEMS
WORDS OF LOVE

© 1985 Judy Piatkus (Publishers) Limited
First published in 1985 by Judy Piatkus
(Publishers) Limited, London

Reprinted 1985

British Library Cataloguing in Publication Data
Cainer, Jonathan
Love signs.
1. Astrology   2. Interpersonal relations
I. Title
133.5'8302   BF1729.15/

ISBN 0–86188–315–2

Designed by Ken Leeder
Typeset by Phoenix Photosetting, Chatham
Printed and bound at The Bath Press, Avon

CONTENTS

1   ARIES (♈ Mar 21–Apr 20)

6   TAURUS (♉ Apr 21–May 21)

11   GEMINI (♊ May 22–Jun 22)

16   CANCER (♋ Jun 23–Jul 23)

21   LEO (♌ Jul 24–Aug 23)

26   VIRGO (♍ Aug 24–Sept 23)

31   LIBRA (♎ Sept 24–Oct 23)

36   SCORPIO (♏ Oct 24–Nov 22)

41   SAGITTARIUS (♐ Nov 23–Dec 21)

46   CAPRICORN (♑ Dec 22–Jan 20)

51   AQUARIUS (♒ Jan 21–Feb 19)

56   PISCES (♓ Feb 20–Mar 20)

When two people become lovers, they enter a private world of their own. In that magical place, there is nothing but an overwhelming sense of belonging. In one sense, love *is* forever. A relationship may fail or fade but the timeless moments when two became one will never be forgotten. The famous couples in this book have all shared moments of deep personal intimacy (not necessarily physical). Some of these relationships have withstood the test of time, while others have blossomed and died.

No Sun sign is 'ideally suited' to any other. To know whether like will seek like, or if opposites attract or repel, an astrologer must study the complete horoscope of both parties.

The dates given in this book are approximate (they change slightly from year to year) but there is no such thing as being 'on the cusp'. If in doubt, read both signs to see which one applies to you.

Each sign is given a general description and is followed by series of comments describing how they feel about you. To see how you feel about them, read the comments following your own sign.

Each relationship is followed by two symbols. A ♥ describes the likelihood of sexual attraction, a ♥ the potential for a happy long-term union. The highest score is 4; the lower the number the harder you may have to work to overcome your differences. (But don't forget that some of the best things in life are achieved with a little effort!)

♥ ♥ ♥

ARIES

ELEMENT: Fire
SYMBOL: Ram

QUALITY: Cardinal
RULING PLANET:
Mars

'I am'

ARIES is ruled by Mars, the 4th planet from the Sun. Mars takes just over 2 years to complete one cycle of the zodiac. This means that Arians will often experience subtle changes of mood or energy every two months (the time it takes Mars to move through a sign) and find that much of their life is subject to revision at bi-annual intervals.

By tradition, Mars is a 'malefic' planet, the God of war, ruling confrontation and danger. Today, we understand it to be a 'motivating force' providing those born under its influence with energy and determination. Mars harmonises well with Venus, Pluto and Mercury. Less harmonious is Mars with the Moon, Uranus or the Sun.

Arians have little time for introspection or social niceties. They take each day as it comes and work hard to make the very most of it. If they are outspoken, it's because there's so much to say and so little time to say it in. If they are fiery, it's because they have little affinity with detail and tend to grab a flame thrower to clear what they perceive as undergrowth. A head-on approach has its obvious drawbacks. The Arian needs to master the arts of patience and foresight. This is no easy task for a person who instinctively feels that there's 'no time like the present' (and even that may be a bit too late!).

Never down for long, rarely without hope, always ready to try something new, Arians are dynamic, positive and, when tempered by experience, wise. Arians are ideally suited to people less impulsive than themselves. At the same time, they mustn't and shouldn't fall in love with anyone who can't stand the heat of their intense, immediate, spontaneous outbursts.

Rams are horny animals with strong impulsive desires. Once you have aroused their interest, they will pursue you to the ends of the earth. Once you have let them catch you, prepare to be engulfed in a raging inferno. They are energetic, enthusiastic lovers and sometimes need to be taught to relax and discover a gentler way of loving.

THE ARIES MALE is essentially quick off the mark. If he could only learn the merest modicum of forethought there would be few to rival him. Without it, he may be a danger to those around him. There is so much inner confidence emanating from him that it is hard to resist assuming that he must be right and should be followed. As a lover he is uncomplicated, uncompromising and (surprisingly) unselfish. You may need plenty of stamina to keep up with his constant need for stimulation but he has a lot to give and you'll find his vibrancy infectious.

♥

THE ARIES FEMALE pays the piper and calls the tunes. At least, she *ought* to. Sometimes her conditioning may lead her to suppress her own power and strength and project it instead on to others. This is a dire mistake. She *must* recognise the implications of her own strength, or lovers will fast become old friends as she hunts incessantly for the impossible goal; a partner who has more strength than she. She is headstrong in love; not to be found coyly hiding in a corner awaiting a suitor. If she sees a potential mate she will leave them in no doubt about her interest! Whether they can maintain it for her is another matter and depends mainly on whether they can give as good as they get.

ARIES AND . . .

. . . ARIES
A box of firecrackers without a lid. One stray spark will set the whole lot off! ♥♥♥♥♥

. . . TAURUS
Very exciting initially, but there will be differences which will be hard to resolve. ♥♥♥♥♥

. . . GEMINI
This relationship has a very high *interest* rate, but can be subject to sudden fluctuations. ♥♥♥♥♥

. . . CANCER
If you'll fly them to the moon, they'll build you a stairway to the stars! ♥♥♥♥♥♥♥

. . . LEO
Do they wrap you round their little finger, or are you keeping them under your thumb? ♥♥♥♥♥

. . . VIRGO
Virgo won't pull the wool over your eyes (but you'll have to take it out of your ears). ♥♥♥

. . . LIBRA
You'll be (L)ost! (I)nfatuated (B)y their (R)adiant (A)ttraction. Or it could spell disaster! ♥♥♥♥♥♥

. . . SCORPIO
The lemon tree is very pretty, but the fruit of the lemon is very much an acquired taste. ♥♥♥♥♥

. . . SAGITTARIUS
The great freedom fighter meets an escapologist. Neither of you will change tactics. ♥ ♥♥

. . . CAPRICORN
What a formidable team! (You had better invest in some hefty bedsprings!) ♥ ♥ ♥♥ ♥ ♥

. . . AQUARIUS
It will take a very determined battering ram to break down the walls to this city. ♥ ♥♥

. . . PISCES
A seductive proposition but you must learn to tread carefully on their dreams. ♥ ♥♥ ♥

♥

ARIES LOVERS

♈ + ♈   Steve McQueen + Ali McGraw
♈ + ♉   David Steel + Judy Steel
♈ + ♊   Jane Asher + Gerald Scarfe
♈ + ♋   Michael Parkinson + Mary Parkinson
♈ + ♌   Desi Arnaz + Lucille Ball
♈ + ♍   Billie Holiday + Lester Young
♈ + ♎   Bonnie (Parker) + Clyde (Barrow)
♈ + ♏   Clementine + Winston Spencer Churchill
♈ + ♐   Joan Crawford + Douglas Fairbanks Jnr
♈ + ♑   Willis Hall + Jill Bennet
♈ + ♒   André Previn + Mia Farrow
♈ + ♓   Eddie Fisher + Elizabeth Taylor

TAURUS

ELEMENT: Earth   QUALITY: Fixed
SYMBOL: Bull   RULING PLANET:
    Venus

'I value'

TAURUS is ruled by Venus, the closest planet to our own. By tradition, Venus is a 'benefic' planet, the goddess of love, ruling fertility and material wealth. Today, she is seen as a 'creative' force, showering artistic talent and refinement on those born under her influence. Venus takes about 1 year to complete 1 cycle of the zodiac and, because she is nearer than us to the Sun, in the birth chart she is never more than 2 signs ahead or behind the sun-sign itself. Venusian individuals will harmonise well with those born under the influence of almost any planet, but have a special affinity with Jupiterian and Lunar people and *may* find life harder with Martian or Plutonian people. (See also Libra.)

You'll rarely find a Taurean in a hurry. These people have class. It doesn't matter where they are or what they're doing, they bring a stylish grace to everything they do. For some people, patience is a virtue. For Taureans, it's an obsession. That's why they make such fine artists, musicians or craftspeople. They have an instinctive feel for the fruits of the Earth. It makes them materialists in the nicest sense of the word. They love and cherish all things bright and beautiful and will often own collections of rare and wonderful objects, lovingly maintained in pristine condition.

Their refined creativity keeps them in great demand. They like to mull things over and take life at a gentle (though not leisurely) pace. All this may sound more like the china shop than the bull, but if you're in any doubt about the aptness of the Taurean symbol, watch them when the black mood descends. When pushed beyond their natural limits, a raging bull appears, devastating anything that crosses its path. Nobody, but nobody, sulks like a frustrated Taurean.

Their lovers are delicate treasures to be gently caressed until they achieve the pinnacle of ecstacy. It's an addictive experience, which is just as well, for Taureans don't often waste time with people they don't intend to cherish for a long time. Be careful, however, that you don't end up as just part of their collection, gathering dust on a shelf.

THE TAURUS MALE is the original Mr Cool. This guy is so laid back, it's a wonder he doesn't topple over. He's normally a snappy dresser and a smooth mover and you'll see him in the most fashionable nightspots, grooving into the small hours. At work, by refusing any project he can't handle, he appears calm and composed at all times. Needless to say, it's an act. Actually he is nervous, moody and shy but he's born blessed with this supine gracefulness that makes his clumsiest movements seem choreographed. In private, he's very much in need of reassurance, and thrives on physical contact. *You'll* rarely find him without a lover whom he can impress with his carefully honed sexual technique, but *he'll* rarely find a lover who will take him beyond it.

♥

THE TAURUS FEMALE is very difficult to dislike. She's affable, amenable and attractive. If she has a fault, it's probably the fact that she's annoyingly 'together', like the lady on the TV commercials whose washing is always whiter than white. Not that she's necessarily domesticated. It's just that she has this amazing way of making things look easy. Part of the secret of her success is the way she vets all potential suitors until she finds someone who will aid and abet her bid for consumate efficiency. Such a partner finds her deeply sensual touch simply an added bonus!

TAURUS AND . . .

. . . ARIES
Life on the edge of a volcano. Taurus smoulders, while Aries erupts. ♥ ♥ ♥ ♥ ♥

. . . TAURUS
Actually, you're not too stubborn at all. It's *they* who must learn to give way! ♥ ♥ ♥ ♥ ♥

. . . GEMINI
Locked in a room with a bluebottle, Taurus finds the novelty soon wears off! ♥ ♥ ♥ ♥

. . . CANCER
You can't be faint-hearted, there's too much mouth-to-mouth resuscitation going on!
♥ ♥ ♥ ♥ ♥ ♥ ♥ ♥ ♥

. . . LEO
They'll dig their heels in and stay their ground. (So will you.) ♥ ♥ ♥ ♥ ♥

. . . VIRGO
This is a very creative union. Virgo creates a fuss, Taurus creates an escape route. ♥ ♥ ♥ ♥

. . . LIBRA
There *is* considerable potential here if you can convince Libran's to consider a bull! ♥ ♥ ♥ ♥ ♥ ♥

. . . SCORPIO
Odd, how you can be so close and yet so far apart.
♥ ♥ ♥ ♥ ♥

. . . SAGITTARIUS
This bright elusive butterfly of love needs a Taurus with a very large net to catch it. ♥ ♥ ♥ ♥ ♥

. . . CAPRICORN
Like concrete re-inforced with steel, your love is sturdy, steady and strong. ♥ ♥ ♥ ♥ ♥ ♥ ♥

. . . AQUARIUS
This would be rather like trying to keep a DC10 in the backyard; pointless without a runway. ♥ ♥ ♥ ♥

. . . PISCES
An easy relationship to fall into; hard to climb out of. ♥ ♥ ♥ ♥ ♥ ♥ ♥

♥

TAURUS LOVERS

♉ + ♈	Bjorn Uldaeus + Agneta Fallskog (ABBA)
♉ + ♉	Tessa Wyatt + Richard O'Sullivan
♉ + ♊	Czar Nicholas II + Czarina Alexandra
♉ + ♋	Desmond Wilcox + Esther Rantzen
♉ + ♌	Gary Cooper + Clara Bow
♉ + ♍	Jill Ireland + David McAllum
♉ + ♎	Denis Thatcher + Margaret Thatcher
♉ + ♏	Lawrence Olivier + Vivien Leigh
♉ + ♐	Bing Crosby + Kathryn Crosby
♉ + ♑	Corretta Scott + Martin Luther King
♉ + ♒	Henry Fonda + Margaret Sullivan
♉ + ♓	Robert Browning + Elizabeth Barrett

GEMINI

ELEMENT: Air
SYMBOL: Twins

QUALITY: Mutable
RULING PLANET:
Mercury

'I think'

GEMINI is ruled by Mercury. The closest planet
to the Sun (and hence the fastest), Mercury takes
under a year to complete its astrological cycle and
in the birth chart it will never be more than 1 sign
ahead or behind the sunsign. In Greek mythology,
Mercury was Hermes, winged messenger of the
gods and became synonymous with all forms of
communication. Hermes was considered neither a
'male' nor a 'female' influence (hermaphrodite)
primarily because sexual interests mattered less
than those involving communication, thought and
travel. As with Venus, those born under Mercury's
influence get on well with most people but there is a
special affinity for Uranians and a difficulty with
those of a Plutonian nature. (See also Virgo.)

Geminis are often described as childlike. It's true that they have an enthusiastic hunger for information and a bubbly style of expression, but don't mistake this for innocence or simplicity. Moodier or more complex people would be hard to find. It really does seem as though there are two separate personalities battling it out inside one head!

This certainly explains the Geminian versatility, but it also raises the serious problem of 'identity'. How can you know what you want from life if you don't know who you are? Too often these emotional Peter Pans fail to resolve this basic question. Instead, they spend their lives dabbling. A little bit of this. A little bit of that. And what (I hear you ask) about a little bit of the other?

Somehow, sex (and love) demands an involvement in the adult world that most Geminis are loathe to give. To protect themselves from the seemingly terrible fate of commitment, they resort to flippancy and flirtation. Some Geminis change partners more often than other people change socks.

The good news is that if you can actually catch one of these butterflies, you'll find that they suddenly lack the motivation to escape. Then, as long as you can provide plenty of novelty and keep up with their conversations, you'll have a bright, even brilliant partner who will remain devoted and loyal in the face of all adversity.

THE GEMINI MALE can be spotted a mile away. His head is in the clouds and his foot is in his mouth! The voice in his head rarely takes a rest and he often becomes a slave to his own power of analysis. There are 17 sides to every story and he can see them all. It can be a crippling disadvantage when he needs to make a simple decision, but it's also his greatest potential talent. He's never short of good ideas and new ways of looking at life. Still, a genius in one field can be a fool in another – he must learn to concentrate his talent where it will be most effective. In love, he is looking for an angel. Someone patient, soft and strong, who will put up with his immaturity, ignore his moodiness and encourage his sporadic outbursts of inspiration.

♥

THE GEMINI FEMALE has a tough choice. Naturally endowed with a bright, bubbly personality it's easy for her to adopt a trivial and vacuous disguise. Then, nobody need notice how deeply she thinks. She's always got a thousand burning questions to be answered. She likes to keep her finger on the pulse of things, and as a result, is sometimes accused of being either bossy or nosy. Sex, for her, is also about communication. The more things she can discuss, the longer the relationship may last. There will come a point where she has talked and listened enough. Then her heart will suddenly open and her mouth will suddenly shut.

GEMINI AND . . .

. . . ARIES
A Gemini is already full of hot air. Add it to Arian fire and you'll either take off or explode! ♥ ♥ ♥ ♥ ♥

. . . TAURUS
They could turn your wild ideas into concrete realities, but you'll have to learn patience. ♥ ♥ ♥ ♥

. . . GEMINI
The phone company will fund its annual Xmas party with the profit on your bill! ♥ ♥ ♥ ♥ ♥ ♥

. . . CANCER
They'll demand an emotional commitment which you may find hard to give. Don't fake it! ♥ ♥ ♥ ♥

. . . LEO
With their beauty and your brains you make a good team! Just keep flattering them. ♥ ♥ ♥ ♥ ♥ ♥ ♥

. . . VIRGO
(V)ariety, (I)nterest, (R)apport, (G)rowth and (O)pportunity. Not just initial promise. ♥ ♥ ♥ ♥ ♥ ♥

. . . LIBRA
You'll live happily ever after in a world of analysis and conjecture. ♥ ♥ ♥ ♥ ♥ ♥

. . . SCORPIO
On offer: a brand new perspective on life with fantastic lover. Sincere Geminis only need apply.
♥ ♥ ♥

. . . SAGITTARIUS

This is always an affair, never a relationship. They share your fear of mundanity. ♥ ♥ ♥♡ ♥ ♥

. . . CAPRICORN

Their no-nonsense approach can be a little off-putting. You may feel hemmed in. ♥♥♡ ♥ ♥

. . . AQUARIUS

Whoever said 'There's nothing new under the sun' forgot about what Geminis get up to with Aquarians! ♥♥ ♥ ♥♡ ♥ ♥ ♥

. . . PISCES

Like an oasis in a desert: cool and refreshing. Just make sure it's not a mirage. ♥ ♥♥♡ ♥

GEMINI LOVERS

♊ + ♈	Douglas Fairbanks Snr + Mary Pickford
♊ + ♉	Prince Philip + Queen Elizabeth II
♊ + ♊	Nanette Newman + Bryan Forbes
♊ + ♋	Tony Curtis + Janet Leigh
♊ + ♌	Joan Collins + Maxwell Reed
♊ + ♍	Queen Victoria + Prince Albert
♊ + ♎	Paul McCartney + Linda McCartney
♊ + ♏	Cole Porter + Linda Lee Thomas
♊ + ♐	Maud Gonne + W B Yeats
♊ + ♑	Richard Wagner + Cosima Wagner
♊ + ♒	Lee Majors + Farah Fawcett
♊ + ♓	Judy Garland + Vincente Minelli

CANCER

ELEMENT: Water   QUALITY: Cardinal
SYMBOL: Crab   RULING PLANET:
Moon

'I feel'

CANCER is ruled by the Moon. The Moon circles the Earth not the Sun. It governs the tides of the oceans and our emotions. From the dawn of humanity, the Moon has been a symbol of mystery and magic. Today, we consider her a 'maternal', protective and essentially 'receptive' influence governing our 'subconscious' minds. Once every 27.5 days, the Moon completes a cycle in the zodiac (taking just over 2 days in each sign). This is one reason why those who feel its influence strongly are often subject to rapid changes in mood. Another is, of course, the visible phases that appear on her face. Lunar individuals will find a special affinity with those born under Venus, Pluto and Neptune and may find less immediate empathy with Solar or Uranian personalities.

On the whole, these people have an unassuming manner. Don't be fooled. They are as sharp as stainless steel scissors! Admittedly, their insight is instinctive rather than analytical but, particularly when it comes to people, they rarely miss a trick.

This immaculate judgement of character is their greatest asset. It's similar to the way a good mother knows her children. Traditionally, the sign Cancer symbolises maternity. Both males and females have this powerful desire to nurture, cherish and protect. They love to 'look after' their loved ones and there's little they won't do for them. Naturally this makes them loyal and loving. But woe betide you if you play with a Cancer's emotions. Remember that their trust is genuine and comes from a heartfelt emotion, not a false sense of morality. That's why they are so often on the defensive. Like a crab, retreating into its shell, Cancerians protect themselves by shutting out anything that could be potentially hurtful, harmful or horrid.

In some parts of the world, because of the unfortunate associations with the word 'Cancer' astrologers have taken to calling these people 'Moon Children'. Only Cancers could be so sensitive as to need this tactful re-christening! Nonetheless, it may be fitting, for it is at night when the Cancerian familiarity comes into its own. Like teddy bears, they are always ready to kiss and cuddle away the darkness.

THE CANCER MALE has strong maternal instincts. He can't physically *have* children so instead he adopts attitudes and jealously guards them. You'll rarely find a Cancer man without strong opinions, for they allow him to hide some of his gentle, compassionate nature from the world. People are forever taking advantage of his generous nature and it sometimes seems as though the only way he can protect himself is through evasion. Once you've won his respect, he'll take all your troubles on his powerful shoulders and do everything he can to make you feel loved and wanted. All he hopes for in return is honesty in life, passion in bed, and fidelity in love.

♥

THE CANCER FEMALE has a very deep need for reassurance. She really wants to feel loved, needed and appreciated. To disguise this, she will often put on a brave show of strength, initiative and 'guts'. This, if you like, is the hard shell of the crab disguising a soft, anxious and vulnerable underbelly. Which side she displays really depends on how much she trusts you. Getting involved with her can be like returning to the womb! She will surround you with love and protection. Where, mentally, she can be reserved and cautious, physically she is warm, demonstrative and sexually adventurous. Be warned, though: in return for this orgy of affection you must give her faithful love and unwavering support.

CANCER AND . . .

. . . ARIES
A Cancer can go a long way on a kiss and a promise.
Aries will take you there for the promise of a kiss.

♥ ♥ ♥ ♥ ♥ ♥ ♥

. . . TAURUS
You've both got hearty appetites for food as well as
each other.

♥ ♥ ♥ ♥ ♥ ♥ ♥

. . . GEMINI
Just be sure that it's true when they say 'I love you'
– It's a cinch for them to tell a lie.

♥ ♥ ♥ ♥

. . . CANCER
A very cosy couple. Roasting chestnuts by the fire,
curled up in each other's arms

♥ ♥ ♥ ♥ ♥ ♥ ♥ ♥

. . . LEO
A brave Cancer will find a lot to love here but
should keep their head out of the lion's mouth.

♥ ♥ ♥ ♥

. . . VIRGO
Nervous Nellie meets worried Will, possible *if* you
could stop feeding each other's insecurity.

♥ ♥ ♥ ♥ ♥

. . . LIBRA
Shut your eyes and count to 10. Are they still
there? If so, it may be worth trying.

♥ ♥ ♥ ♥ ♥

. . . SCORPIO
You are two figures silhouetted against the setting
sun, lost in a world of your own.

♥ ♥ ♥ ♥ ♥ ♥ ♥ ♥

. . . SAGITTARIUS
You can't be serious! (But as long as you're not, you'll really enjoy this while it lasts.) ♥ ♥ ♥ ♥♥

. . . CAPRICORN
Moody young crab and grumpy old goat, you'll stomp and mutter your way to happiness.

♥ ♥ ♥ ♥ ♥

. . . AQUARIUS
At first they may seem to be a little aloof, but you can soon change all that. ♥ ♥♥ ♥ ♥

. . . PISCES
Ideal drinking partners. You can drown your sorrows together . . . and find plenty to celebrate.

♥ ♥ ♥ ♥♥ ♥ ♥

♥

CANCER LOVERS

♋ + ♈	Glenys Kinnock + Neil Kinnock
♋ + ♊	Edward VIII + Mrs Simpson
♋ + ♋	Linda Ronstadt + Gerry Brown
♋ + ♌	Joséphine Beauharnais + Napoleon Bonaparte
♋ + ♍	Henry VIII + Anne of Cleves
♋ + ♎	Jerry Hall + Bryan Ferry
♋ + ♏	Delaney + Bonnie Bramlett
♋ + ♐	Michael Williams + Judi Dench
♋ + ♑	Kris Kristofferson + Janis Joplin
♋ + ♒	Natalie Wood + Robert Wagner
♋ + ♓	June Carter + Johnny Cash

LEO

ELEMENT: Fire   QUALITY: Fixed
SYMBOL: Lion   RULING PLANET:
Sun

'I protect'

LEO is ruled by the Sun, centre of our solar system. The Sun is 109 times larger than the Earth and we take 365¼ days to travel around it. As we move through the heavens, it 'appears' as though the Sun is tracing a circle around the Earth, and it is by dividing this circle into 12 equal sections that we measure the signs of the zodiac (*not* from the stars). 'Sunsigns' have become popular partly because they vary little from year to year and partly because the Sun is a fundamental life-giving force of obvious importance. It is a powerful, uncomplicated and vital energy and those born under its influence will share these qualities. They will also have a special, symbiotic relationship with the Moon, and a healthy ambivalence to all other planets.

21

Leo is the ultimate sunsign. By astrological tradition, the Sun is 'at home' in this region of the zodiac. Perhaps that's why most Leos are so confident and presumptious. This, in turn, may be why so many people wrongly dismiss them as arrogant, selfish show-offs.

In truth, they are no more arrogant than anyone else – just more blatant and vociferous about their opinions. Certainly they are not selfish (a Leo will give you his last crust without a second thought), and, as for show-offs, well it's true that Leos like attention but they're very careful about how they earn it, and before taking the stage they'll make sure they've got something worth watching. In fact, if there *is* a Leonine vice, it must be pride. They have a regal bearing and go to great lengths to protect their dignity.

When it comes to matters of the heart, Lions prefer to hunt than be hunted. You may offer them gifts and generally pay them homage, but rest assured that if they want you, you will be summoned! Once you receive the call, be careful never to act as if you own them. In private, they like you to hold them tight; in public, they value their independence and prefer you to take your place with the rest of their admirers. Occasionally Leos will throw back their heads and emit a deafening roar. Ignore it – the time to worry is when they're too quiet!

THE LEO MALE certainly doesn't believe in wasted action and will lie patiently in wait of opportunities. Then, suddenly, without warning, he will stretch himself out and pounce on his prey. You don't argue with this man unless you enjoy a fight. The idea that he may be wrong is hard for him to grasp! This same 'blind romanticism' extends into his love life. If he loves you at all, he'll become totally fixated and move heaven and earth on your behalf. He makes a fiery and impulsive lover, and a playful but fickle mate.

♥

THE LEO FEMALE. Ink and paper are not fit mediums to describe this awesome being. Statues hewn in gold would fall short of encapsulating her majesty. She is simply a divine goddess who deigns to grace us mere mortals with her presence. Needless to say, her lover should be of similar calibre. Sadly, too often, her handsome prince will turn out to be a well-dressed frog! Before you accept an invitation to the royal bedchamber, make sure you have seen through the regal image and know her for the lovable little girl she really is. Otherwise, you may find yourself a loyal servant of the crown, dutifully warming the sheets until a more perceptive suitor arrives.

LEO AND . . .

. . . ARIES
Plenty of passion but look out: they can give (almost) as good as they get! ♥ ♥ ♥♡ ♥

. . . TAURUS
Taureans appreciate the finer things in life. How can they fail to resist you? ♥ ♥ ♥♡ ♥

. . . GEMINI
Fluttering round you like moths at a flame, if they get their wings burnt, are you to blame? ♥♥♥ ♥ ♥

. . . CANCER
You'll see a show of unexpected strength from these usually soppy people. It's attractive. ♥ ♥ ♥♡ ♥

. . . LEO
Occasionally this is splendid. But usually no town is big enough for the two of you. ♥ ♥♡♥ ♥

. . . VIRGO
Are you ready to be taken to pieces and put back together? If in doubt, stay away. ♥ ♥♡ ♥ ♥

. . . LIBRA
It's easy to fall for the charm, but much harder to live with the continual confusion. ♥ ♥ ♥ ♥♡ ♥

. . . SCORPIO
They get a trial by fire; you get to skate on thin ice. Fatal but unavoidable! ♥ ♥ ♥♡

. . . SAGITTARIUS
If only you could slow them down to a reasonable pace, they'd be the perfect partner. ♥ ♥ ♥ ♥ ♥

. . . CAPRICORN
Between the sheets they get your vote; everywhere else, they get your goat! ♥ ♥ ♥ ♥ ♥

. . . AQUARIUS
They certainly make you feel strongly. What is less certain is whether you feel love or hate. ♥ ♥ ♥ ♥ ♥ ♥

. . . PISCES
There's only one question hanging over this relationship – your place or theirs? ♥ ♥ ♥ ♥ ♥ ♥ ♥

LEO LOVERS

♌ + ♈ Eddie Fisher + Debbie Reynolds
♌ + ♉ Peter O'Toole + Sîan Phillips
♌ + ♊ Jackie Onassis + John F Kennedy
♌ + ♋ Mick Jagger + Jerry Hall
♌ + ♌ Princess Margaret + Roddy Llewellyn
♌ + ♍ Percy Bysshe Shelley + Mary
　　　 Wollstonecraft Shelley
♌ + ♎ James Hill + Rita Hayworth
♌ + ♏ John Derek + Bo Derek
♌ + ♐ Jill St John + Frank Sinatra
♌ + ♑ Phil Spector + Ronnie Spector
♌ + ♒ Clara Bow + Eddie Cantor
♌ + ♓ George Sand + Frédéric Chopin

VIRGO

ELEMENT: Earth   QUALITY: Mutable
SYMBOL: Harvest   RULING PLANET:
Goddess   Mercury

'I understand'

VIRGO is ruled by Mercury, as is Gemini. Both signs share an 'intellectual' approach to life, appropriate to the god of communication and thought, but there are marked differences between Mercury's influence in Virgo and its influence in Gemini. Gemini is an Air sign, and here Mercury is free and unfettered, wandering at will between different points of interest. Virgo is an Earth sign, and here Mercury becomes more interested in specific detail, finding rhyme, reason and patterns and giving them practical expression. Both signs are 'mutable' (i.e. they find it easy to accept change), but again the difference between Air and Earth means that Virgos do so less easily (see also Gemini).

The symbol for Virgo is not 'a virgin' but a beautiful woman clutching a sheaf of wheat, a fertility symbol most fitting for this productive Earth sign. Virgos are the most remarkably perceptive and creative people. No sign of the zodiac has more insight, intelligence and discrimination. Virgos would easily be the most dangerous and powerful people on the planet were it not for one thing: they can become terribly introverted.

The Virgo's power of analysis is supposed to be used for the good of humanity and when all that perspicacity is focused on themselves, they become crippled. It can be so easy for them to gauge the potential ramifications of a given situation that they become too self-conscious to initiate anything. Often they will leave first moves to those with less foresight than themselves. With an impeccable eye for detail and a strong sense of duty, they often wind up in responsible but unexciting professions. This by no means makes them boring. It's just that, even in times of reckless abandon, they've got a corner of one eye fixed on the brakes and can, if necessary, pull themselves together at a moment's notice. That's not boring . . . that's brilliant!

Lovemaking, for a Virgo, is not a brief exchange of heated passion but a sensual marathon of mounting excitement. Relationships should in theory be easy, but for some reason they can find it hard to be demonstrative.

THE VIRGO MALE has a hard time of things. His insight reveals many truths, and his conscience forces him to tell them. He has what our grandparents used to call moral fibre. He also has a taste for trouble. The more potential problems his lover has (whether internal or external), the more he is drawn to the liason. This is strange, because actually the very act of opening up to emotional commitment is enough to threaten his stable view of life. It seems that he is perpetually involved with the problems of people less organised than himself, and to them he brings his incisive mind and gentle sense of humour.

♥

THE VIRGO FEMALE is the Earth Mother to end all archetypes, as gentle as she is strong, and as clever as she is open-minded. Not that she is perfect, although she tries to be! She tends to be self-sacrificing to the point of martyrdom. You'll rarely find her in the spotlight. She prefers to hide behind the scenes, efficiently providing essential support while others take the bows. Enjoying the thrill of adventure but lacking the courage to instigate it, she is often drawn to rash but inspired individuals. While basking in their reflected glory, she will fail to notice if they walk all over her. When eventually she opens her eyes, she will inevitably also find that someone with a better offer has been patiently waiting.

VIRGO AND . . .

. . . ARIES
The constant activity is entertaining. It's the
constant arguing that exhausts you. ♥ ♥ ♥ ♥ ♥

. . . TAURUS
You'll find it hard to make them understand that
you have more to offer than your body! ♥ ♥ ♥ ♥ ♥

. . . GEMINI
They always have plenty to tell you, but rarely have
time to listen. ♥ ♥ ♥ ♥ ♥ ♥

. . . CANCER
It sometimes seems like this relationship is very
much give and take. You give, they take.
♥ ♥ ♥ ♥ ♥ ♥

. . . LEO
Leos make everything into a melodrama. You
worry enough already without their extra help!
♥ ♥ ♥ ♥ ♥

. . . VIRGO
No-one understands a Virgo like a Virgo. Is it all
too good to be true? ♥ ♥ ♥ ♥ ♥ ♥ ♥

. . . LIBRA
This can work well. You often arrive at similar
conclusions for different reasons. ♥ ♥ ♥ ♥ ♥ ♥

. . . SCORPIO
You know that they know, but they don't know
you know they know! It's hard work! ♥ ♥ ♥ ♥

. . . SAGITTARIUS

You'll enjoy their optimism. They'll listen to your wisdom. Together you're invincible. ♥ ♥ ♥ ♥ ♥ ♥

. . . CAPRICORN

You find them a little stubborn. They find you a little fussy. This could be a little problem! ♥ ♥ ♥ ♥

. . . AQUARIUS

This great intellectual rapport has difficulty establishing a physical base. ♥ ♥ ♥ ♥ ♥

. . . PISCES

You can learn a lot from your illogical, emotional opposite if you make the effort. ♥ ♥ ♥ ♥ ♥

♥

VIRGO LOVERS

♍ + ♈	Greto Garbo + Leopold Stokowski
♍ + ♉	Elliot Gould + Barbra Streisand
♍ + ♊	John Kennedy Snr + Rose Kennedy
♍ + ♋	Anne Bancroft + Mel Brooks
♍ + ♌	D H Lawrence + Frieda Weekly
♍ + ♍	Florence Eldridge + Frederic March
♍ + ♎	Margaret Trudeau + Pierre Trudeau
♍ + ♏	Johnny Dankworth + Cleo Laine
♍ + ♐	Sophia Loren + Carlo Ponti
♍ + ♑	H G Wells + Rebecca West
♍ + ♒	Jeremy Irons + Sinead Cusack
♍ + ♓	Joan Kennedy + Edward Kennedy

LIBRA

ELEMENT: Air
SYMBOL: Scales

QUALITY: Cardinal
RULING PLANET:
Venus

'I evaluate'

LIBRA is ruled by Venus, as is Taurus. Both signs
share a 'creative' and 'aesthetic' approach to life but
as with Virgo and Gemini, Taurus is an Earth sign,
while Libra is an Air sign. In this instance, the
difference between Earth and Air means that
Taureans find it easier to give strong, physical
expression to their creative instincts (they may
sing, sculpt or carve) whereas Librans have a
lighter, more intellectual, approach to their talent
and often appreciate colour and style more than
shape and texture. Also, Taurus is a Fixed sign
whereas Libra is a Cardinal sign. The Fixed signs
are notorious for their determination and tenacity,
whereas the Cardinal signs are known to be better
at getting things started than seeing things
through. (See also Taurus.)

If it seems that Librans float effortlessly through life, it's because they aren't weighed down with the sense of urgency that most of us have. Their main consideration is to be where 'there never is heard a discouraging word and the skies are not cloudy or grey.' They like life to be peaceful and harmonious and go to great lengths to keep it that way. It's very difficult to argue with a Libran. They'll *discuss* anything and everything, but you'll rarely find them taking a point of view and defending it. If they do, it's most likely to be about something that offends their aesthetic judgement or threatens the tranquillity of their home.

The old chestnut about Libran indecisiveness is not really true. Those born under the sign of the only machine in the zodiac (the scales) *can* make up their minds, but most of them take a little longer than the rest of us to weigh up the pros and cons. They have a scrupulous commitment to fair play, and as a result you can be sure that any choices they make will be well thought out.

Libra is about sharing. These people don't usually like to be alone and yearn for a perfect partner who will help them create their heaven on earth. To help them attract one, they have a sort of deceptively innocent and slightly dizzy way about them. Don't be fooled. They can be wickedly sensual and responsive. Though many may fall for the Libran charm, few will live up to their exacting specifications.

THE LIBRA MALE falls into two distinct types. The first is a man of style, who can be overbearing and insensitive. The second is a rather bland character who will do anything for a quiet life. Both these personalities stem from a difficulty in making snap decisions. The first makes too many, the second too few. They both, however, have expensive tastes and can be a little too concerned with keeping up appearances. They also are both talented and creative in one form or another. This man is looking for a partner to merge with. He is normally courteous and charming, attracting many admirers. Unfortunately, too many of them love his body, not his mind. Like all the Air signs, he too requires an intellectual union to bring out his best.

♥

THE LIBRA FEMALE possesses an acute sensitivity. She is a delicate and gentle soul but she sticks out for what she knows is right. Colour and taste are very important to her and her aesthetic eye is infallible. She also carries out her search for a partner in the same discriminating fashion. It can be very hard to know where you stand with her as a lover. She has a habit of saying maybe, whether she means yes or no. The only way to find out is to sneak a gentle kiss and watch her reaction. Then you'll find out in no uncertain terms!

LIBRA AND . . .

. . . ARIES
You're looking for some peace of mind, but they're looking for a piece of the action! ♥ ♥ ♥ ♥

. . . TAURUS
Wherever it is you're heading for, having a Taurus on board helps you get there quicker!

♥ ♥ ♥ ♥ ♥ ♥ ♥

. . . GEMINI
You can't judge a book by the cover. Once you pick this one up, you'll never put them down. ♥ ♥ ♥ ♥ ♥

. . . CANCER
You like their emotional outlook, but it can be a little overwhelming. ♥ ♥ ♥ ♥

. . . LEO
Leave your worries on the doorstep. Just direct your feet to the sunny side of the street. ♥ ♥ ♥ ♥ ♥ ♥

. . . VIRGO
Plenty to talk about, plenty to think about, plenty to like about this thoughtful person. ♥ ♥ ♥ ♥ ♥ ♥

. . . LIBRA
How could two such aware, discriminating people possibly fail to adore each other? ♥ ♥ ♥ ♥ ♥ ♥

. . . SCORPIO
You'll find them intense, they'll find you woolly. They'll get bored, you'll get hurt. ♥ ♥ ♥

... SAGITTARIUS
Very interesting. They like to do things on a grand scale. You *are* a grand scale. ♥ ♥ ♥ ♥ ♥

... CAPRICORN
Like driving a car with the handbrake on: safe, slow, but a bit wearing. ♥ ♥ ♥ ♥ ♥

... AQUARIUS
You'll discover things you never knew were possible. They'll think it's you. You'll think it's them. ♥ ♥ ♥ ♥ ♥ ♥

... PISCES
They irritate you. You annoy them. It will take a lot of loving to overcome this. ♥ ♥ ♥ ♥

LIBRA LOVERS

♎ + ♈ Dory Previn + André Previn
♎ + ♉ Ray Brown + Ella Fitzgerald
♎ + ♊ Anthony Newley + Joan Collins
♎ + ♋ Harold Pinter + Vivien Merchant
♎ + ♌ Julie Andrews + Blake Edwards
♎ + ♍ Britt Ekland + Peter Sellers
♎ + ♎ Oscar Wilde + Lord Alfred Douglas
♎ + ♏ Dwight Eisenhower + Mamie Eisenhower
♎ + ♐ Diana Dors + Alan Lake
♎ + ♑ Carol Lombard + Howard Hughes
♎ + ♒ John Lennon + Yoko Ono
♎ + ♓ Rachel Roberts + Rex Harrison

SCORPIO

ELEMENT: Water   QUALITY: Fixed
SYMBOL: Scorpion   RULING PLANET:
Pluto

'I desire'

SCORPIO is ruled by Pluto. Furthest from the Sun (3,670 million miles) and therefore the slowest moving planet, Pluto takes up to 17 years to move through 1 *sign* of the zodiac. In Greek mythology, Pluto was Hades, the dark lord of the underworld. Today, Pluto has become synonymous with the process of transformation and change. All things secretive, taboo or sexual come under its jurisdiction. This, perhaps, is where the Scorpionic reputation for 'intensity' comes from (although until 1930, when Pluto was discovered, Scorpio was actually ruled, like Aries, by Mars). Plutonians have a special relationship with those born under the influence of Mars, the Moon and Neptune, and difficulty with those of a Mercurial, Venusian and Solar disposition.

Of all the signs in the zodiac, Scorpio gets the worst publicity. Astrologers totally misunderstand these powerful, passionate people. In truth, Scorpios are neither sex-mad, vicious or vengeful. They are deeply sensitive souls who are too perceptive for their own good. Most of us are prepared to live in a world that's fuzzy round the edges. Scorpios need things to be clear cut. They must know where they stand and who they stand there with.

The Scorpio mind is fascinated by all the things that nice people don't talk about. They believe in magic, are proud of their sexuality and not afraid of death. The sting in the Scorpion's tail is only used in self-defence. Their real weapon is a frank, piercing sense of humour. In our mixed up, bottled up society it's often the only way they can communicate.

The Scorpio heart is a live volcano. When it erupts, few can withstand its force. They are protecting themselves and you when they hold back their feelings.

Romance for a Scorpio has nothing to do with hearts and flowers. To them, sex is a sensual pleasure but love is a four-letter word (it spells fear). It's not hard to seduce a Scorpio (though it's hard to resist being seduced *by* one!). To win their trust is a lifetime's work, but few things could be more rewarding.

37

THE SCORPIO MALE is desperately afraid of being hurt. He has learned the hard way that few can take him as he really is. Our world is full of cardboard cut-out stereotypes. There is no image to fit the Scorpio male. He is neither moronically macho (he feels, cares and cries) nor an insipid intellectual (too much passion, power and presence). In an attempt to hide the richness of his spirit he pretends to be invincible. It makes him attractive to the wrong people. Sex is never hard for him to find. Understanding is almost impossible. To make a Scorpio male happy, you must see right through the façade and nurture his suppressed sensitivity.

♥

THE SCORPIO FEMALE values honesty above all else. She detests hypocrisy and refuses to operate dual standards. It's not that she's a goody goody. On the contrary, she has little time for conventional morality. She's a very rare sort of lady; one who is not afraid to speak her mind and stay her ground. Her sexual presence is almost awe-inspiring, and along with her strength it disguises her vulnerability. Deep down inside, she is open and innocent. She longs to be guided not followed. Her lover must combine integrity, sensitivity, warmth and spontaneity. With him, she may be taken to any extreme but never for granted.

SCORPIO AND . . .

. . . ARIES
You love to win, they hate to lose. It will work if
you can find a common cause to fight. ♥ ♥ ♥ ♥ ♥ ♥

. . . TAURUS
Most people spend one third of their life in bed.
You two will probably spend much longer.

♥ ♥ ♥ ♥ ♥

. . . GEMINI
Co-existence *is* possible but you'll need to wear
earplugs and they'll need a suit of armour. ♥ ♥ ♥

. . . CANCER
You'll fly on the wings of love – take-off may be
slow but touchdown is rare. ♥ ♥ ♥ ♥ ♥ ♥ ♥

. . . LEO
Some unions are made in Heaven. This one is made
in Hong Kong. It falls apart too easily. ♥ ♥ ♥ ♥ ♥

. . . VIRGO
They think they can read you like a book. It makes
you want to throw the book at them. ♥ ♥ ♥ ♥

. . . LIBRA
You'll probably find them very attractive but lacking the substance you need. ♥ ♥ ♥ ♥

. . . SCORPIO
When this is good, it's very very good. But when
this is bad it's *horrid*! ♥ ♥ ♥

...SAGITTARIUS
Like drinking champagne. (Very exciting but the bubbles may get up your nose.) ♥♥♥♡♡

...CAPRICORN
They'll have a tendency to get on top of you. (But you probably like that sort of thing!) ♥♥♥♥♡

...AQUARIUS
The irresistible force meets the immovable object. Surely one of you must give. (!?!) ♥♥♥♥

...PISCES
(P)assionate, (I)nteresting, (S)ensual, (C)aring, (E)lectric, (S)pell-binding. ♥♥♥♥♡♡♥♥♥

SCORPIO LOVERS

♏ + ♈	Katherine Hepburn + Spencer Tracy
♏ + ♉	Marie Curie + Pierre Curie
♏ + ♊	Grace Kelly + Prince Rainier
♏ + ♋	Prince Charles + Princess Diana
♏ + ♌	Sylvia Plath + Ted Hughes
♏ + ♍	Marie Antoinette + Louis XVI
♏ + ♎	Bruce Welch + Olivia Newton John
♏ + ♏	Edward VII + Lillie Langtry
♏ + ♐	Ike Turner + Tina Turner
♏ + ♑	Lulu + Maurice Gibb
♏ + ♒	Eleanor Roosevelt + Franklin D Roosevelt
♏ + ♓	Jack Haley Jnr + Liza Minelli

SAGITTARIUS

ELEMENT: Fire
SYMBOL: Centaur

QUALITY: Mutable
RULING PLANET:
Jupiter

'I hope'

SAGITTARIUS is ruled by Jupiter, 5th planet from the Sun. Jupiter (Zeus in mythology) is sometimes known as the Santa Claus of the solar system, bestowing hope, happiness and talent on those born under its influence. Jupiter takes around 12 years to complete a cycle of the zodiac, which means that its natives will be sensitive to a new, positive charge of energy each year as Jupiter moves into a new sign. It is also the largest planet in the zodiac – which nicely reflects the Sagittarian reputation for 'expansiveness'. The magnaminity of Jupiter means that there are few planets it cannot blend well with, but there is perhaps a special affinity for Neptune and Mercury and a certain antipathy towards natives of Saturn.

Sagittarians are not interested in being 'understood'. Most of them rarely stay in one place long enough to let it happen. Those who do are far too busy for introspection.

They are easy to please. If you've got a dragon to slay or a mountain that needs climbing, give them a call. If you're looking for someone to share the quiet life with, don't bother! It's not that they'll refuse (the word *no* is not in a Sagittarian vocabulary), it's just that if they're bored they'll start inventing challenges. Even a simple country walk will turn into an obstacle race. (Why walk round the fence when you can leap over it?) What they lack in caution, tact and reserve, they make up in enthusiasm, honesty and buoyancy. They take their phenomenal luck for granted and push it to the limit. Annoyingly, they get away with it. There will always be 'close scrapes' and 'near misses' but things have this uncanny way of working out all right in the end – and Sagittarians make the most of it!

Centaurs don't fall in love, they tumble. They love with an all-consuming passion and will do anything to win the affection of their chosen flame. Often, they are more interested in firing their arrows than hitting the target. Unless you are capable of leaping headlong into wild adventure at a moment's notice, you will only keep a Sagittarian's interest by remaining somehow unobtainable, aloof or mysterious.

THE SAGITTARIUS MALE needs to feel free, but he doesn't always know it. Sometimes, he *thinks* he would like the challenge of responsibility. He is actually capable of this, but at great cost. With a brave smile on his face, he slowly sinks into the quagmire of commitment while his optimism and *savoire faire* dissolve in the mud. If you love him, you should remember this when he swears undying allegiance. He is sexually excited by romantic fantasy and can pluck unbridled passion from thin air. Before you respond with similar gusto, be sure you can tell the difference between a kiss and promise. The latter will only prove valid if you hold his hand, not his feet!

THE SAGITTARIUS FEMALE has a brilliant imagination and normally leads a lifestyle to match. You'll rarely find her darning socks or cleaning cupboards. More likely, she'll be engaged in a great journey of discovery that may take her to the ends of the Earth and back. She has a tendency to bite off more than she can chew and may, for example, decide to right the wrongs of a cruel world *single-handedly*. Once her heart is set on a quest like this, little will stop her. In love, she is not quite so un-inhibited. Sexual encounters often lead to a loss of freedom and she is keen to protect her independence. She must find a lover who is light-hearted, spontaneous and adventurous, or she will love you and leave you for someone or something less constraining.

SAGITTARIUS AND . . .

. . . ARIES
When a poor second fiddle meets first violin, one must bow out while the other tunes in. ♥♥♥

. . . TAURUS
You'll be elated by their sensual, earthy nature, but frustrated by their need to feel secure. ♥♥♥♥

. . . GEMINI
Always something to say, rarely nothing to do, never a dull moment. ♥♥♥♥♥♥

. . . CANCER
Like sinking in quicksand – irresistible but a bit constricting! ♥♥♥♥♥

. . . LEO
What an ideal match! The slightest spark provokes a flame. (Let go before your fingers burn!) ♥♥♥♥♥♥

. . . VIRGO
Don't be fooled by the front. If you're lucky enough to win their love, they'll bring you *real* adventure! ♥♥♥♥♥♥

. . . LIBRA
In an *ideal* world this would be a perfect relation-ship . . . ♥♥♥♥♥♥

. . . SCORPIO
This mixture of fire and water makes for steamy nights and stormy days! ♥♥♥♥

. . . SAGITTARIUS
Nothing on earth could keep you apart; nothing in heaven could keep you together. ♥♥♥♥♡♡♡

. . . CAPRICORN
You'd better be sure. The road to hell is paved with good intentions. ♥♥♥♡

. . . AQUARIUS
You share a love of freedom but differ on how to achieve it. ♥♥♡

. . . PISCES
What a way to go! Making love on the backseat while careering downhill at 110 mph. ♥♥♥♥♡♡

SAGITTARIUS LOVERS

♐ + ♈ Hope Lange + Alan Pakula
♐ + ♉ Greg Allman + Cher
♐ + ♊ Joe Dimaggio + Marilyn Monroe
♐ + ♋ Edwina + Earl Mountbatten
♐ + ♌ Alfred de Musset + George Sand
♐ + ♍ Chris Evert Lloyd + John Lloyd
♐ + ♎ Pat Phoenix + Tony Booth
♐ + ♏ Benny Andersson + Frieda Fredericksson (AΒBA)
♐ + ♐ Pamela Stephenson + Billy Connolly
♐ + ♑ Frank Sinatra + Ava Gardner
♐ + ♒ Woody Allen + Mia Farrow
♐ + ♓ Betty Grable + Harry James

CAPRICORN

ELEMENT: Earth　　**QUALITY:** Cardinal
SYMBOL: Sea goat　**RULING PLANET:**
Saturn

'I organise'

CAPRICORN is ruled by Saturn. The 6th planet from the Sun, Saturn (Cronus in Greek mythology) may be thought of as Old Father Time – teaching its natives the lessons of restraint and discipline. Saturn takes about 27.5 years to complete a zodiacal cycle and, as well as experiencing a major upheaval each time Saturn returns to its place at the time of birth, Capricorns may also find testing times once every 7 years as Saturn 'squares' or 'opposes' its natal position. The 'function' of Saturn is to bring an awareness of limitation which, used positively, makes its natives practical and, used negatively, makes them unduly pessimistic. This grounding influence blends well with Uranus and Mercury, but may take longer to be successful with Jupiter and Neptune.

The phrase 'down to earth' must have been invented to describe these people. They have more common sense to offer humanity than it deserves! Every project they undertake, no matter how lofty or esoteric, will have a logical purpose and a practical result. In a world of dreamers, here are the realists. A pessimist may call a cup half empty; an optimist, half full. A Capricorn calls it 50% liquid, 50% air! This commitment to truth does not always endear them to others. They can be inexorably blunt about what they think and what they want! Life is too short to waste with waffle.

Having a direct approach naturally brings its own rewards. There are few problems that a Capricorn won't see a simple solution for. There are also very few people who can pull the wool over their eyes. Nonetheless, it *can* happen. It's a mistake to consider them invulnerable.

The mythological goat has a fish's tail and Capricorns often find themselves swimming in the ocean of emotion. For them, the act of love is not just a tactile indulgence to be relished, but a meeting of souls to be cherished. Although they prefer not to admit to this weakness, it exists and can serve to cloud their usually infallible judgement. The mysteriously erotic lover who attracts them is often the annoyingly erratic partner who eventually confounds them. To avoid this, they must either develop greater emotional awareness or become less intellectually intractable!

THE CAPRICORN MALE's uncompromising approach can be a little tiresome in daily life, but in times of stress his invincible strength is a splendid asset. Give this man a problem to solve or a project to organise and he'll deal with it efficiently and quietly. Give him a relationship to deal with and he'll go quietly potty. People, unlike things, are neither predictable nor straightforward, and though he finds this frustrating he will, given time, make the effort to adjust. When in love, he may not shower you in flowers and finery, but if you want to be appreciated, involved and devoured in an earthquake of sensual passion – stay aboard.

♥

THE CAPRICORN FEMALE. With a cool head attached firmly to elegant shoulders, she gives the world an impression of consumate efficiency. In fact, she is really a mischievous schoolgirl with a love of pranks and parties. It's a shame she's ashamed of this side of her character. There's nothing wrong with a little irresponsibility, particularly when she's normally so careful. In other respects, this sophisticated lady knows what she wants and how to get it. She doesn't dwell in fantasy but while she's not looking for a knight in shining armour, she certainly likes nights of wine and *amour*. Once you have gained her trust, she will respond to physical affection with almost outrageous abandon!

CAPRICORN AND . . .

. . . ARIES

Thunder and lightning. You two will get on just fine but the rest of the world had better look out!

♥ ♥ ♥ ♥ ♥ ♥

. . . TAURUS

Like two comic strip heroes who win every battle, together you are successful but rather predictable.

♥ ♥ ♥ ♥ ♥ ♥

. . . GEMINI

This one might run and run. If it doesn't, you will, and as far away as possible!   ♥ ♥ ♥ ♥

. . . CANCER

They want to smother you but you don't really like it.   ♥ ♥ ♥ ♥

. . . LEO

You're unlikely to be awestruck by their majesty. They ought to respect you for it.   ♥ ♥

. . . VIRGO

Two shrewd operators on the same patch.   ♥ ♥ ♥ ♥

. . . LIBRA

They'll open you up to a whole new world of colour and gaiety, if you don't shut them out.   ♥ ♥ ♥ ♥ ♥

. . . SCORPIO

Terms of endearment in the short term; terms of reference need redefining in the long term.

♥ ♥ ♥ ♥ ♥ ♥

. . . SAGITTARIUS
Your high expectations don't measure up to their high aspirations. ♥♥♥♥♥

. . . CAPRICORN
There are few things that you two can't manage between you. Except perhaps frivolity. ♥♥♥♥♥♥♥♥

. . . AQUARIUS
If you know what's good for you, you'll take this up if it's offered and ask if it's not. ♥♥ ♥♥♥ ♥♥

. . . PISCES
Their dreamy mysterious eyes will turn you on, don't undervalue their instinctive approach. ♥♥♥ ♥♥

CAPRICORN LOVERS

♑ + ♈	Diane Keaton + Warren Beatty
♑ + ♉	Steve Stills + Judy Collins
♑ + ♊	Howard Hughes + Marilyn Monroe
♑ + ♋	Les Paul + Mary Ford
♑ + ♌	Walter Mondale + Joan Mondale
♑ + ♍	Lady Bird Johnson + Lyndon B Johnson
♑ + ♎	Ava Gardner + Mickey Rooney
♑ + ♏	Moira Shearer + Ludovic Kennedy
♑ + ♐	Jill Bennet + John Osborne
♑ + ♑	Cary Grant + Dyan Cannon
♑ + ♒	Jane Wyman + Ronald Reagan
♑ + ♓	Chairman Mao + Mrs Mao

AQUARIUS

ELEMENT: Air   QUALITY: Fixed
SYMBOL: Water bearer   RULING PLANET:
                              Uranus

'I know'

AQUARIUS is ruled by Uranus. Seventh planet
from the Sun, Uranus was discovered in the 18th
century by the astronomer William Herschel.
Coinciding with this discovery came revolutions in
France and America and for this reason Uranus has
become associated with spontaneous outbursts of
inspirational passion. This, it seems, is more fitting
for the Aquarian temperament than the colder
image portrayed by its former ruler Saturn. The 84
years it takes Uranus to complete 1 cycle of the
zodiac make its 'squares' and 'oppositions' (every
21 years from birth) a crucial time of re-assessment
for those born under its influence. Uranian people
are well suited to those born under Saturn and
Mercury, but not so well matched with Neptune or
Mars.

There's something about Aquarians that makes them hard to generalise about. It's partly because they're so individualistic. It's partly because as we enter the Aquarian age, their role in our world is changing. It's also partly because the symbol of water bearer is misleading: Aquarius is an Air sign.

Most people form their opinions from a 'gut reaction'. First they 'feel' something, then they rationalise their experience. For Aquarians, this process works in reverse. As a result, most of the time they are cool and level-headed; their feelings are just as strong and deep, but it takes more to stir them up. They reserve their tears and temper for the defence of a utopian vision. Each Aquarian has a longing to make the world a better place. As few people understand this sort of motivation, Aquarians are often thought of as unpredictable, eccentric or just plain odd! Their ability to swing from laughter to stern sobriety at a moment's notice doesn't help either!

As a friend of an Aquarian, you can consider yourself very special. No-one chooses their companions more carefully. If you have an Aquarian lover . . . Well sex for an Aquarian is always an extension of intellectual rapport. When this is missing, no amount of emotion will compensate – a robot would give you more warmth. On the other hand, if your love affair *is* based on a meeting of minds, you will never have a more sensitive, gentle or considerate lover.

THE AQUARIUS MALE has an intellectual arrogance that makes him refuse to listen to advice. He may be often right, but his preference for rational rather than instinctive judgements means that, in rising above the maze of human emotions, he misses a world of experience. His inherent eccentricity is reflected in his love life. It is never predictable. His love of novelty and experiment means that he will either have many weird and wonderful affairs, or one adventurous and very open-minded partner! His lovers may feel that, even in the most passionate situations, he is only half with them. His long-term partner will discover that the aloof individual they first met gradually turns into a caring, spontaneous and exciting spouse.

THE AQUARIUS FEMALE is a human dynamo. Buzzing with energy and ideas, she knows what she wants and usually gets it. She dares to be different and pays little attention to the comments and criticisms of others. Even so, she has a winning way which makes her popular. She knows how to play the game of social interaction almost too well. She can be surprisingly matter-of-fact about sex, offhand about love and indifferent to affection. It's all an act. She's just terrified of opening floodgates that may not shut at her command. She may have many trysts, but till she finds someone who can see right through her 'superior attitude' she will never have truly had a lover.

AQUARIUS AND . . .

. . . ARIES
You already live life close to the edge. Are you sure you can take this extra push? ♥ ♥ ♥

. . . TAURUS
You will feel like a bird in a beautiful cage. ♥ ♥ ♥ ♥

. . . GEMINI
Two deep, original thinkers. You can both retire to the clouds and count silver linings. ♥ ♥ ♥ ♥ ♥ ♥ ♥ ♥

. . . CANCER
This will be very cosy once you overcome your initial fear of being loved. ♥ ♥ ♥ ♥ ♥ ♥

. . . LEO
As long as there are parties to go to, this is a great team – otherwise, fire and ice . . . ♥ ♥ ♥ ♥ ♥ ♥

. . . VIRGO
They'll earth you without bringing you *down* to earth. It's worth letting them do it! ♥ ♥ ♥ ♥ ♥

. . . LIBRA
'Makes you feel like spring is sprung. Bells to be rung and a *wonderful* fling to be flung!' ♥ ♥ ♥ ♥ ♥ ♥

. . . SCORPIO
Sense vs Sensuality. Ration vs Passion. You may prefer a ringside seat to going 10 rounds! ♥ ♥

. . . SAGITTARIUS

There's a *quelque chose* about their *savoir faire* which inspires a *je ne sais quoi. Comprend?*   ♥ ♥ ♥

. . . CAPRICORN

Take one Capricorn every night before retiring. If symptoms persist – increase the dose!   ♥ ♥ ♥ ♥ ♥ ♥ ♥ ♥

. . . AQUARIUS

(A)lthough (Q)uite (U)npredictable (A)s a (R)elationship, (I)t's (U)nusually (S)uccessful.   ♥ ♥ ♥ ♥ ♥ ♥

. . . PISCES

There's a big difference between a visionary and a dreamer. It may be insurmountable.   ♥ ♥ ♥ ♥

♥

AQUARIUS LOVERS

♒ + ♈	Claire Bloom + Rod Steiger
♒ + ♉	Farah Fawcett + Ryan O'Neal
♒ + ♊	Vanessa Redgrave + Tony Richardson
♒ + ♋	Ronald Reagan + Nancy Reagan
♒ + ♌	Simon Mackorkindale + Susan George
♒ + ♍	Humphrey Bogart + Lauren Bacall
♒ + ♎	Roger Vadim + Brigitte Bardot
♒ + ♏	Graham Nash + Joni Mitchell
♒ + ♐	Virginia Woolf + Leonard Woolf
♒ + ♑	Ben Lyon + Bebe Daniels
♒ + ♒	Carole King + Gerry Goffin
♒ + ♓	Paul Newman + Joanne Woodward

PISCES

ELEMENT: Water   QUALITY: Mutable
SYMBOL: Fishes   RULING PLANET:
Neptune

'I dream'

PISCES is ruled by Neptune. The 8th planet was discovered in the last century and has become firmly associated with 'illusion' and 'dreams'. Under its jurisdiction fall film-making, psycho-analysis and all things that are not quite what they seem. The power of creative imagination that lies in our subconscious often contradicts the world of rationality and logic, and yet, without it, there can be no spiritual growth. Those born under Neptune's influence have a special part to play in unleashing this force. Neptune's progress through the zodiac is slow – up to 14 years in each *sign*. Change for a Piscean is stimulated often enough by internal pressure, regardless of the position of their ruling planet. Neptune blends well with Jupiter and the Moon – not so easily perhaps with Saturn or Uranus.

Pisceans can be wonderfully nebulous. When threatened, the two fishes swim in different directions, dissipating the argument by agreeing with both sides. In the absence of a rose-tinted world, Pisceans wear rose-tinted spectacles! To anyone else, this may seem like escapism. For a Pisces, it's an act of faith. Dreamers are the people who shape tomorrow; the space age was envisaged not by scientists but by writers of science fiction. Those who can see the potential inherent in mankind are to be cherished and encouraged, and protected from their vulnerability.

It seems that everyone who needs a shoulder to cry on or someone to confide in selects one of these approachable people. Unfortunately, Pisceans tend to absorb all this emotional energy rather like sponges, and eventually it seeps out in the form of nervous energy and a desire to retreat into the world of their imagination. This is why Pisceans are often prone to abuse drink or drugs. They love to over-indulge their senses, and in love they are greedy too.

A lovestruck Piscean wants to indulge in a fairy-tale escape from the bricks and mortar of their surroundings, to retreat with their beloved to a high castle on a white horse through misty fields and enchanted forests. As in all fairy tales, there will be goblins, dragons and danger along the way but, as in all fairy tales, a happy ending is inevitable.

THE PISCES MALE has one of life's most valuable possessions: an open mind. He also has something difficult for a male to come to terms with: genuine sensitivity. It makes him soft, gentle and compassionate. Fortunately, he is rarely bothered by the ignorant notion that 'toughness' equates with strength. His heart is lighter than the air, his smile is brighter than the sun, but he has weaknesses on as grand a scale as his talents. As you disappear with him into a secret world of gentle erotic discovery, remember that he's as impetuous as he is demonstrative, and as gullible as he is inspired. If the bubble is not to burst, you must give him support as well as love.

THE PISCES FEMALE is an incurable optimist. She doesn't tempt fate, she taunts it from the safety of her ivory tower. To her concerned lover, it seems that she is constantly under attack. Rarely will you meet someone with more apparent problems. If she ever opens her eyes wide enough to perceive the external perspective, she may panic too. But only momentarily. As long as she clings to her dreams she is safe, for in them she sleepwalks along a tightrope of potential disaster as if it were a fortified bridge. To love this lady, you must be prepared to dive deep into the realm of magic. In the flickering firelight, your eyes will meet and her body will envelope you in an all-consuming embrace from which there may never be a return.

PISCES AND . . .

. . . ARIES
They'll sweep you off your feet. Just be careful you
don't end up getting brushed off!　　　♥♥♥♥♡♡

. . . TAURUS
If it feels good – do it! (Not that you two will need
any telling!)　　　♥♥♥♥♡♡♡

. . . GEMINI
Walk with them – and a thousand violins begin to
play. You get misty whenever they're near!
　　　♥♥♥♥♡♡

. . . CANCER
Very emotional: years of tears and laughter filled
with months of magic and moonlight.
　　　♥♥♥♥♡♡♡

. . . LEO
They can be very warm when it suits them, but not
always when it suits you.　　　♥♥♥♥♡♡

. . . VIRGO
You may need an interpreter at first, but you'll
soon learn to speak their language.　　　♥♥♡♡♡

. . . LIBRA
You never seem to know whether you're coming or
going with them. Probably plenty of both!　　　♥♥♥♡

. . . SCORPIO
(S)exy,　　(C)aring,　　(O)bdurate,　　(R)elatable,
(P)romiscuous, (I)nviting, (O)utrageous!
　　　♥♥♥♡♡♡♡

. . . SAGITTARIUS
Every day's a grand adventure, every night's a grand affair, every one's a winner! ♥♥♥♥♡♡♡

. . . CAPRICORN
There are limitations to this relationship and you will be better off if you stick within them. ♥♥♡♡

. . . AQUARIUS
You two are cut from different cloths. Only a very clever tailor could make you a suit. ♥♥♡♡

. . . PISCES
'The mate that fate had you created for . . . It's that old black magic called love!' ♥♥♥♥♡♡♡♡

♥

PISCES LOVERS

♓ + ♈	Patti Harrison + Eric Clapton
♓ + ♉	Tom Courtenay + Cheryl Kennedy
♓ + ♊	Rex Harrison + Lilli Palmer
♓ + ♋	James Taylor + Carly Simon
♓ + ♌	Lord Snowdon + Princess Margaret
♓ + ♍	W H Auden + Christopher Isherwood
♓ + ♎	Trish Van Devere + George C Scott
♓ + ♏	Elizabeth Taylor + Richard Burton
♓ + ♐	May Britt + Sammy Davis Jnr
♓ + ♑	Sir Harold Wilson + Mary Wilson
♓ + ♒	Liza Minelli + Peter Allen
♓ + ♓	Duchess of Kent + Duke of Kent